VIA Folios 77

THE OTHER COLORS IN A SNOW STORM

THE OTHER COLORS IN A SNOW STORM

Richard Vetere

BORDIGHERA PRESS

Library of Congress Control Number: 2012935976

Printed in the United States.

Published by
BORDIGHERA PRESS
John D. Calandra Italian American Institute
25 West 43rd Street, 17th Floor
New York, NY 10036

VIA FOLIOS 77
ISBN 978-1-59954-039-9

Once again for Lisa!

ACKNOWLEDGEMENTS

"Global Amnesia" first appeared in *Slipstream* (New York); "Human Sacrifice" first appeared in *Orbis* (Wicker, England); "Two Sides to Every Story" and "John and Mary Six Pack" appeared in *Cobweb* (London); "Skill" first appeared in *Hybrid* (Durham, England), and "The Moon in the Mirror" in *Black Buzzard Review* (North Carolina); "The Other Colors in a Snow Storm" and "The Rest of My Life" appeared in 2 *Bridges Review*. "A Dream of Angels" first appeared in *A Dream of Angels*, published by Northwoods Press in 1984.

Mr. Vetere's two earlier books of poetry are *Memories of Human Hands* (Manyland Books 1976) and *A Dream of Angels* (Northwoods Press 1984).

TABLE OF CONTENTS

GLOBIAL AMNESIA

They say they are my parents
but I don't know who those people are.
Her hair sticks up like she was caught in a hurricane
and he's drunk and smells of booze.
The room they keep me in is supposed to be mine
when I was growing up. I don't remember having a room.
I don't remember growing up.
They say I came to a church to get out of the rain.
They say the newspapers call me "John Doe."
I tell them I like "Mister President" better.
When we talk I prefer to call it a 'news conference.'
They keep me locked in the house so I call out.
I call the mayor, the governor and Chinese take-out.

Old girlfriends call and say I'm faking it.
They say it would be impossible not to remember *them*.
The government sent me a tax form.
The credit card company sent me bills.
The city sent me a parking ticket.
The church sent me a reminder for donations.
My ex-wife had her lawyer call for alimony payments.
I even got a chain letter.

I prefer to be put under stress because
I don't remember charging anything.
I don't remember earning an income.
I don't remember saying "I love you" for the wrong reason.

I'm no different than anyone else.
I forgot that people die for their beliefs.
I forgot Viet Nam.
I forgot how banks red-line a neighborhood
then lend billions to serial killer dictators
who treat their loans like bets at a crap table.
I forgot there are twenty thousand nuclear missiles
aimed at my apartment.
I forgot someone killed thirty women in Texas
then had a book written about his hard life
and his painful upbringing.
I forgot Barbara Cousins who died of cancer in fourth grade.
I forgot that I kissed her and told her
that I would remember that kiss forever.

The other night I heard on the radio
how the demographic of New Yorkers is changing.
I don't remember being part of a demographic.
In fact, I'm not here.
I'm at Columbia University 1968.
My hair is long, grown out of principle.
A thousand faces like mine have eyes the color of light
because we see everything.
I have books under my arm
and ancient symbols drawn on my denim jacket.
It was then that faces fresh with anticipation
lured the sun down from the gods again,
but like amnesia, came the Red Sea
covering the universe as the gold American Express card
replaced the peace sign.

 "Mister President! The world would like a word with you,"
some stranger says to me.
I give him a stare as indifferent as John Doe's needs
are to Congress.

Tomorrow, I'll forget how to speak.
I'll forget that the world has my body.
I'll forget that I'm a prisoner of its memories.

THE OTHER COLORS IN A SNOW STORM

Orange is a lit window in the dark
or a rooftop on the other side of the sky.
The colorless sound of a dog's bark
or an oriole on a branch before it flies.
There's a fireplace glowing on the hill
where imagined strangers sit around and talk.
I was one of them once, a long time ago,
standing at an open door, watching it snow.

Blue is the snow on the fields at night
and the cars on the highway passing by,
and the color of your eye when you flash on a light
and the moon rising in the sky.
I never see much red in the winter months
except for the sun rising above my bed.
Can you feel the wind as you dream?
Does it matter what all the colors mean?

White is the darkness that never goes away
stretching to the horizon in the middle of the night.
White is the glare of a thousand years of day
burning with the illusion of a warm, lingering light.
I remember you laughing as we lay in the snow
helpless as the world tilted for an afternoon.
What are the other colors in a snow storm?
What moments do we choose to shed, or to mourn?

The rainbow lives in a driving wind
though everyone else is tucked away safe inside.

You were once right here, where it all began,
waiting for your clothes as they dried.
I wonder who else sees only the snow
blasting through the heavy, hungry air?
What separated you from me, and everything else?
Where do all the colors go, after all the colors melt?

TWO SIDES TO EVERY STORY

There are two sides to every story.
Here's mine: when I was five years old
he was tall, handsome, and easy-going.
When I was seven he hit batting practice
every Saturday for the Little League baseball team
to protect me from the coach's son
who was a bully.
When I was eleven he broke all the rules
and brought me hamburgers in the hospital
sneaking into my room in the dead of the night
with a wild, courageous smile on his face.
When I was thirteen, he pushed me to get up and dance
with grown women to help me fight my shyness.
When I was seventeen, he cursed my drinking calling me a "bum"
telling me my long hair looked "stupid"
and that my need to write "would never get me anywhere."
"You'll die sitting in front of the TV!" I yelled at him
once when I was nineteen.
He cried when I moved out.
When I was twenty-six he wondered what was wrong with me
that my life didn't make any sense to him.
"When are you getting married?" he consistently asked me
then told me he "felt sorry for any women I was with."
When I was thirty-three he wondered 'why' I was so insecure
and why I couldn't get close to any one woman.
Then he asked me if I was a homosexual.
When he was sixty he asked me "How was I capable of doing
all the things I did?" He was impressed with my mind
for politics, people, my theater acting, the women in my life.

But he called my writing "cold" and told me that if he wrote
his writing would be warm and sensitive.
When he was seventy and dying of cancer
he stared at my strong, healthy body
never saying a word.
"No one will come to my wake," he told my mother.
I made sure everyone I knew stood at his grave
at his funeral.

Here's his: I was his first born
and he cherished me.

SCREENWRITER BLUES

Writing a screenplay is like living in hell,
my apartment is buried in scripts I can't sell.
I still owe the Writers Guild monthly dues.
My agent couldn't get me any interviews.
I got the screenwriter blues.

The studios spend millions on trash.
What happened to the days of movies like M.A.S.H.?
My agent won't return my phone calls,
he's got me by my writer's overalls.
I got the screenwriter blues.

I feel so funny not making any money.
I know it's not the American way.
But Boggie is dead, Serpico fled
and producers want you to defer your pay.

My last movie grossed millions Variety stated,
but the producers never paid me a dime.
I think they're made of mud and slime.
My agent won't return my phone calls,
he's got me by my writer's overalls.
I got the screenwriter blues.

ON MY 45TH BIRTHDAY

Doing it all over again—
I don't think I could.

Listening to my father warn
"never stand out in the crowd."

Hearing my mother's humiliation
confiding to her seven-year old son
how she couldn't afford a nicer dress
for Joey Parisi's confirmation party.

Teenage girls who had no idea.
Those that did—keeping me up all night.
Feeling them up on the handball courts
after rummaging through pocketbooks
for a quick ten bucks.

Going home
puking on my bedroom walls,
then catching the flu.

Being young
looking down from the roof top
into the cemetery.
Being older
standing in the cemetery
looking up at the rooftop.

Wondering when you left me
if I'd ever get over it.
Then realizing
that others leave, too,
and you never get over it.

My first night alone
in my first apartment.
The first woman who ever told me
she was pregnant.

The first disease that almost killed me.

Listening to my brother's voice
on the message machine:
five messages of despair
shouting to me that his daughter was dead.

Getting up early
on a spring day
to identify my niece
at the coroner's.

Burying my father.

*   *   *

In the dark of dark
I've escaped by the skin of my teeth—
from the gun and the knife.
Sucking pleasure from the nipples
of those needing the same kind of shelter.

In time
writing a mountain of euphoria—
from a table of opulence
flooding my memory.

If you can hear this now
tell your shadow
and all who comfort it
the poet you knew
a hundred years ago
was so very, very fortunate.

IN THE HOUSE MY FATHER BOUGHT, MY MOTHER LIVES ALONE

You have to see it to believe it:
how when you subtract one person
another grows.

Though my father painted every wall
and every door in every room
he let go.

I see myself in this conglomerate of memory
forty years earlier:
racing in from the snow, running up stairs,
hiding in my room, ignoring them both,
cursing their complacency
disowning my brothers
wishing I'd be born to someone else
until I, too, grew older and loved the house.

Now, with a cup of tea at the window,
I try and imagine forty years from this day
amazed by a simple observation—
it's the silence my father feared
that my mother revels in.

WHEN WE FIRST MET

When we first met,
I wanted to give you my eyes, my teeth, my hands.
I asked you to wear my fingers and learn my voice
and memorize how my lips were shaped when silent.
So, you wore my eyes and my hands
and you found some reason to memorize my lips
and learned what my voice sounded like without
my fingers and my teeth.
But when you left
you never gave any of it back.

I hear you still wear my fingers and my eyes,
my teeth and my hands.
Are you a cannibal, or is there something religious
going on here?

HUMAN SACRIFICE

When she left me I paced the floor like a madman.
I hugged the walls and cried like a baby.
I tore my shelves of books apart throwing them
across the room in fits of anger and rage.
When she left I lived like a dying man on the phone
listening to it ring until I fell asleep
with the sun rising white in the sky outside my window.
When she left me I held a loaded gun in my hand
fantasizing how she would react to news of my brains
being blasted crosswise in the front door with her photograph
hanging innocently on the wall above my desk.
When she left me I felt the pain the terminally ill
talk about, jumping out of bed every five minutes
of sleep, wondering if the agony will ever go away.
When she left me I felt as if every living relative
and every close friend had just died an awful death
leaving me sole heir to land struck by drought.
When she left me I felt the terrible wrath of the gods
displeased at me for some heinous crime I had committed.
My life, from that moment until forever,
has become an offering in the name of love.

SKILL

The other night on your living room floor
I was as naked as you were.
I watched where your mouth was and where your hands went
with the same scrutiny with which you watched mine.
When it was over I spent the moments wondering
what extraordinary skill brought us exhausted
half-way across the room from where we started
to the sweaty embrace I found myself in?

Last night in a dream
my ex-girlfriend stuck her pregnant stomach up against my chest
staring up at me with accusing eyes—
"this could have been yours," they said, "if you had developed
some talent for love!"

Between talent and skill I've searched for a balance:
one being a feeling mixed with a driving perception
the other—a slight-of-hand practiced to perfection.
In loving it seems "I have it, then I don't."
On the page it's never fully there.

Exhausted by the weight of potential
I'd rather leave you then explain the difficulties.
In my car, I'll drive through miles of darkness and space,
locked between reflected light and passion,
wondering how far the distance between the talent and skill?
Wondering how long it takes to master a natural ability?

THE ROMANCE OF BETTY BOOP

What do I do with you, Betty Boop?
Do I take you to the movies, or the park,
ride down to the beach after dark?
Do I tell you how I long for romance
and how love only happens by circumstance?
Do I smooth back those short, funny curls
so different from all the other girls?
Do I buy you a new dress, make you a star,
carve *I love you* in the neighborhood bar?
Pretend you were a princess from the past
who has found her prince at long last?

Olive Oil had her Popeye,
she knew what was essential
not spiked heels or perfect lips,
but a can of spinach with potential.
What do I do for you, Betty Boop?
You and me, me and you,
Boop Boop Bee Do.

JOHN AND MARY SIX PACK

I haven't had time to examine the bloodied bodies
printed in the newspaper.
I haven't time to talk to you about the recent collapse
of the bank you kept your money in.
I haven't any time to go out and vote
since it doesn't matter who gets elected.
He will steal from my union.
Pet my dog.
Sleep with his secretary.
Murder some foreigners.
Import cocaine.
Lie on national TV.
Smile for the cameras.
Admit he cheated on his law exams
and get a free vacation with a tall, pretty redhead.
But hey, man, I sure got time to watch *Jersey Shore*
The Housewives of Atlanta, the Giants and Jets.
I don't care if war is around the corner,
I don't have AIDS, my daughter isn't missing and I have my
own driveway.

THE MOON IN THE MIRROR

Half the world is lighting a fuse.
The other half is invisible.
Prophets say history is entering a new phase.
Fanatics say the killing time is full.
Corporations judge everything on the last quarter
but all she remembers is a crescent in the sky
the way its light falls on the quietness below,
a look at her reflection before it disappears.
The imagined are accidents within the dark
revolving around what they can never touch:
A witness to the presence of something brilliant in the night—
a woman recreating herself.

IN REACH

In reach is all that was once treasured
nameless is that fear least often measured
in that place of neither death, star or earth
where a life is valued more than its worth.

Despite the years much is left unlearned
harbored in twilight only to be returned
to a murky dawn etched on a lonely face:
a tarnished remnant from an old embrace.

THE NEED TO WRITE NOVELS

He's thirty-eight but he lost all his hair
five years ago. The hair on his beard is gray
and his face has dried up like the Scarecrow
in the Wizard of Oz.
He spent a year in the army and got married
the week he was back. His two kids crawl
through the living room like targets on his scope.
He worries that he hasn't got enough 'time.'
He worries that his kids will admire Madonna instead of him.
He hated Michael Jackson for a year.
He blames the woman's movement for his work not being published.
He watches every show of *American Idol*
cursing the 'tube' for glamorizing trash.
He worries his daughter will grow up fat and his son gay.
He wonders how long he can keep them children.
He spends his nights rewriting drafts of his life,
gives them titles and calls them novels.

THE TOWER OF BABEL

It all began in a small room in a house full of people.
It all began as he grew awkward, his body fused with energy,
elbows and joints tense with vitality
and eyes that blew off the top of his head.
Learning a language that began at the sight of the city
he was alone, timid, groping and in the distance
all he saw was a future with him groping, timid and alone.
It all began with a thought that he did not belong.
She survived the grip of an indifferent fist around her
and screams that could suffocate in the middle of the night.
The yells her parents cried blasted through the railroad
apartment, as she closed out the world around her.
Her own dark eyes burned darkness through her; darkness
only she could mediate. She survived the grip of the fist.
She survived the mirrors of her own image
locked in the tide of her island in the darkness
aware of how frightfully inadequate her own language was.
It all began with the thought that she was alone
and how desperately she wanted to belong.

When he saw her face he wanted to build a bridge to heaven
and carry everything warm about her to their silence in the stars.
Her eyes saw him as one else ever had.
When *she* heard him speak she felt as if it were the first time
anyone in the world had talked to her at all.
She saw his eyes open up the darkness
into a thousand possibilities she had never known before.
When they touched they held each other tightly
as his thoughts took them a thousand miles away.

He taught her language as definite as her darkness
She latched onto his words as they spirited through the night.
His shoulders became her guardian, her love his anchor.
They settled into oneness, crushing out the ruins that came
before them: her personality lifted him to heights he only dreamed
of, as his thoughts created in her landscapes she had never seen.

With her strength beside him he was ready to build the tower
created by the thoughts that he did not belong.
She fueled that energy with her tremendous longing
to be a part of something other than herself.
They fused themselves together with an intimacy,
a knowledge of each other brutal and real.
He began to mimic her words and phrases
as she made the intense thoughts he had her own.
He memorized the firmness of her body, he could taste her
even in the private moments he had without her.
She struggled with his agonies, trying to understand them
aware, perhaps, that they could never be her own.
Together, they set their sights on the mountain of air before them
laying stone upon stone in their journey to the top.
A man and a woman under clouds of youth and illusion
they wanted to reach some fantasy neither had ever seen.
She wanted his happiness to control her insecurities
and he wanted her to call him a "god."
She allowed him the freedom of his ambitions.
She wanted him to build his pride on the foundation of her heart;
he wanted her to reach up to him forever
praising his vision that he did not belong.
Together they built a tower to their misconceptions
in a language they so secretly kept
from where she survived and he began.

In his reach upward his shoulders shook her shadows.
She found her grip around him constraining his every move.
He tried to pull her up close and sometimes throw her

out of his glory as he reached for more and more.
He found himself in places he never dreamed of
unable to share the view with anyone at all.
He believed that he had created a reason for the tower
that went beyond any reason he had ever known.
He learned more about the heavens and the planet
wondering why she had not gained this knowledge, too.
He questioned why she was with him
and what had she to offer to his 'god' upon the ledge.
She kept her pain to herself from the beginning
not wanting to tell him that she had lived it all through him.
Her silence brought her back to the beginning
as if she travelled nowhere at all.
She didn't want to see him as he was forming
into something only the thin air could create.
He was now a master builder creating towers of illusion
in a world of fantasy she had helped him to make.
She started to choke on the absurdity of his 'glory'
and the needs he shouted slowly made her suffocate.
They screamed at one another as they brought the tower upward
both afraid of the heights they had travelled,
both afraid that they might fall.

When they fell it was their speech that went first.
They had stopped talking to one another.
She no longer believed it mattered that she didn't belong
and once again she felt the indifferent fist around her.
He tried hard to bring her back to the beginning
and make her see what she had once seen before,
when she spoke they could no longer understand one another,
they no longer could control the secret of their speech.
When the tower fell he felt his world topple over
and a thousand agonies stuck him all over again.
He reached for her and tried again to touch her
crying out how desperately he wanted to belong.
He tried to hide the thought forever,

the thought that shaped the tower he had created,
but when he tried it was her face that was all he could remember
and her name that lay silent among the stones at his feet.
She buried his memory in the fury and the rubble
doing what she could always do best,
surviving the indifferent fist around her.
In the language which was her silence hollowed out
from her fears of being seen.

It all began with a thought that shaped the future,
a thought that shaped the personality of the thinker
and a map made of everything the thinker planned.
In the pursuit of that thought he found a lover
who helped him imagine a tower in the sky.
A tower created out of imagination and ambition
with a deep rooted longing to belong.
The city still stands, so does the small room
and the indifferent fist around her and the thought.
But in the pity of a language once kept secret,
they no longer speak.

BACK IN PARIS

They tore down the church under my window to put up another condo.
North Flushing used to be a world of trees and empty sidewalks
now you have to walk two blocks to find a place to park your car.

Car alarms go off in the darkness
swaying the limbs from taller trees
as they blast the stillness.
In the middle of the night I awake in a sweat
wondering if one day, out my window,
skyscrapers will line Northern Boulevard
like a parade of chess pieces no one knows how to move.
I pull down the shade afraid one day I may be among the missing
like in some dictatorship
an enemy of the corporation,
a shadow who walks the streets stealing FM radios from Mercedes.

Back in Paris
the police wear flat hats hunting strangers who put bombs in cars
turning radios into high frequency garbage.
Soon they will put bombs in movie theaters.
And nothing will be real anymore.

MEXICO CITY

In the bright sunlight
a pretty dark-skinned lady
has managed to blast my brains out of my ears
holding me with one hand
while slipping out of her jeans with the other.
After the sun fell,
lying on my back,
I wondered who decided to turn Jackson Heights
into a cocaine market,
why clerks living on cheeseburgers
rule my neighborhood from highway diners
and why the simplest words uttered in the dark
can disease a whole city
when intentions remain hidden.

A DREAM OF ANGELS

Though I walk into the room as a wave
I do not break against the ceiling as a shore
nor empty myself into every corner of the room,
but open slowly to ways in which I sleep.

Though once in tune with the voices in the walls
now I hear a knock of whispers from the floor above
that weigh on my shoulders like the drizzle of the rain;
up from the wind, some envisioned wings.

Though I open like a word silent on a page
I drift with the meaning of every sentence that I hear
and hold close the wings of angels
crowded at my head
and break each neck in my sleep.

THE WORKING MAN

I build walls, one wall for you, one wall for you, one wall between us, many walls among us, one wall around you, one wall around you and one wall to hide and cover me.

I work for work's sake.
I am the working man.

I work day to night and then night to day, five day nights a week.
I sleep and eat between intervals of work.
I know myself better than anyone.
I can speak to myself and get a different answer every time.
I'm not pretty and I'm not ugly.
I'm tan from the sun and white from the dark.
My eyes are small and my head bald.
In my company, I'm relaxed.
I work for money to buy jobs to work at.
When I can't work I get sick
so I go through the motions of work to feel better.
The money I can't spend, I spend on saving it
and the money I save, I spend on spending it.
I'm young now, later I'll be old.
I cannot change.
I am work.

LYRICS INSPIRED BY MARIO LANZA MUSICAL

HOLLYWOOD BOULEVARD

I sign with the studio
and they tell me who I am.
"Drop the weight, fatty."
It's a game, it's a sham.

I jump rope, dance all day.
I'm a star on the big screen.
I'm always somebody I ain't.
How'd I get in this dream?

I played Caruso and got raves.
My Mom said, "It's your destiny."
Got the kinks outa my hair
but it all got the best of me.

Back on Mercy Street
my father drove a trunk.
All my friends died young.
Somehow I got the luck.
My wife pops pills to sleep.
My manager hasn't a clue.
I'm driving down Hollywood Boulevard
being told what to do.

DARK SIDE OF VEGAS

You got movie stars and desert,
cocktails and neon lights.
Blonds to lean on,
and something dark besides the night.

You got blackjack and slots,
'Lonely Marys' and 'Gamglin' Joes.'
Souls that go ramblin'
to where? Nobody knows.

This is no place for an angel,
the heat will melt your wings.
Honey, I've seen it all before,
this guy's here only 'cause he sings.

LONG LOVE, LOVE LOST

Got you in my heart
but I have to let you go.
Laughs bring me to another room
but when I look up, it's the same old moon.

Left you in another city
telling you, "I won't forget."
Strange smiles remind me what's wrong
as lies get me through another song.

I should have left you years ago
telling you it won't work out,
instead of you being a shadow in my day
that can't leave, and can't ever stay.

KNOT ENDINGS

Definition of a knot: Knot (not), n. (ME Knotte; AS Cnotta. A knot) 1. A
lump or knot in a thread, cord, etc., formed by passing one free end
through a loop and drawing it tight, or by a tangle drawn tight. 2. A
fastening made by intertwining or tying together pieces of string cord or
rope. 3. An ornamental bow of ribbon or twist of braid, a cocnade, epaulet.
4. A small group of clusters. 5 something that ties or fastens closely or
intricately, a bond of union; especially the bond of marriage. 6. A problem;
difficulty; entanglement. Syn. – bond, connection, tie, snarl, bunch,
collection, perplexity.

I

One
end
    folds
to the other.
Folding
        an edge
into a
closing
        circle:
            a curve.

II

                  Edges
disappear
into
          roundness
where all angles
                  are
absorbed.
Finally,
a   space
of light
deepens
to
a little
sky.

III

Linear
boundaries
           are
infinite
when
indefinite
           shape
and proportion
overwhelm
           leaving
nothing
to
resist.

IV

Entering
            one
end
from another
entrances and exits
cross
and become
one.

V

No
movement
                restricts
direction;
and direction
is   infinite
as it rises.

VI

Noises
          stop.
Shapes develop
slowly
where sound
will
not.

VII

Opening
out   over
an open

space.

VIII

Toward
a point of
contact,
forms respond
and become
                places.

IX

                                Still.

X

Downward slopes
all
direction.
Corners are tied
and fitted
                into a center
from which we see
the end,
also.

THE REST OF MY LIFE

It starts right here, or so I imagine it does.
Somewhere between ice storms and heat waves
as life-long friends, mostly dead and buried,
do sing-alongs at parties held in my head.
Naps bring me the most vivid images
of women mostly; my mother, long ago girlfriends,
sometimes my brothers make an appearance in the old house.
We're young, jumping around, talking a mile a minute,
doing things we never did,
as real as just now and in minute detail,
exploding across the screen.

Human beings like to create 'start' and 'finish' lines
just so they can stick a price tag on 'time spent.'
But they are arbitrary and never last long.
What does have meaning is the rest of it
facing us like a bowl of pasta.
It all tasted great, the sauce, the meatballs
and the parmesan cheese;
but you left some
and you don't know why.

THE BAPTISM OF GINA NIGIDO

A church in bright sunshine
as smiles beam in this holy place.
Where is this transformation?
Do I see an angel in her face?

Immersed in water, all her sins,
even those not committed yet,
are forgiven and she is blessed
as she emerges from her innocence.

I, too, have been through a change,
a dramatic transformation of the soul,
but what course her life will follow
only she will grow to know.

SESTINA

A building near the sea grows large over the water.
Water runs wild in swells miles out to sea.
Sea-like skies drift high over beaches.
Beaches stretch for years like deserts under the sun.
Sun-like eyes grow dark in the shadows.
Shadows fall beneath the building like mountains.

An arm in the dark is white like a mountain
where a lamp's light falls and scatters like water
and hides in a room , your face in a shadow,
tired in the dark, miles under the sea.
Behind the curtain crawls the heat of the sun
away from the empty walls that cages desert beaches.

Up from the floor, eyes like open like beaches
staring at the buildings, darkness and mountains.
Out from the clouds caught by the sun,
into the needle goes life, air and water.
Water wets blood wetter than the sea:
opened in love, an arm warm to the shadows.

She lies in your arms, half-hid by shadows,
her body is salt and white as the beaches,
her mouth breaths air, wetness and the sea.
as her hands fold high and rise up like mountains.
Nothing in the room says you're in water
but the way light filters in from the sun.

The roof top is wild with wind and sun
as your voice runs up and over the shadows.
You let out a scream like a whisper of water
afraid of the moon's endless stretch of beaches.
Today, you give your sight to the buildings and mountains
and stretch your body like the tides of the sea.

Water runs wild in swells miles out to sea.
Breaches stretch for years like deserts under the sun.
Shadows fall beneath the building like mountains.
Sun-like eyes grow dark in the shadows.
Sea-like skies drift high over the beaches.
A building near the sea grows large over the water.

Tomorrow, you'll fall against her cellar door like water,
Tired in your eyes, you'll find in the shadows,
Mountains that loom large under the sea.

NOTES

ABOUT THE AUTHOR

Richard Vetere was born in New York City. He wrote *The Third Miracle*, published by Simon & Schuster, and subsequently co-wrote the screenplay adaptation for producer Francis Ford Coppola. Agnieszka Holland directed the movie, which starred Ed Harris. Richard also wrote the teleplay adaptation of his stage play *The Marriage Fool*, starring Walter Matthau and Carol Burnett; it was CBS's most watched TV movie.

Richard is also an avid playwright; his plays include: *Caravaggio*; *Machiavelli*; *One Shot, One Kill*; *Gangster Apparel*; and the children's play *Bird Brain*, published by Dramatic Publishing. His previous books of poetry, in turn, include: *Memories of Human Hands* and *A Dream of Angels*. He also wrote the novel *Baroque* (also published by Bordi-ghera Press) and the cult-classic movie *Vigilante*.

The Richard Vetere Collection is at Stony Brook University's Frank Melville Library. Richard teaches playwriting in the Master's program at New York University and film writing at Queens College. He holds a Master's degree from Columbia University.

VIA Folios

A refereed book series dedicated to Italian Studies and the culture of Italian Americans in North America and other areas of the Italian diaspora.

Published by BORDIGHERA, INC., an independently owned not-for-profit scholarly organization that has no legal affiliation to the University of Central Florida or the John D. Calandra Italian American Institute, Queens College, City University of New York.

ROBERT LIMA
Sardinia • Sardegna
Vol. 24, Poetry, $10.00

DANIELA GIOSEFFI
Going On
Vol. 23, Poetry, $10.00

ROSS TALARICO
The Journey Home
Vol. 22, Poetry, $12.00

EMANUEL DI PASQUALE
The Silver Lake Love Poems
Vol. 21, Poetry, $7.00

JOSEPH TUSIANI
Ethnicity
Vol. 20, Selected Poetry, $12.00

JENNIFER LAGIER
Second Class Citizen
Vol. 19, Poetry, $8.00

FELIX STEFANILE
The Country of Absence
Vol. 18, Poetry, $9.00

PHILIP CANNISTRARO
Blackshirts
Vol. 17, History, $12.00

LUIGI RUSTICHELLI, ED.
Seminario sul racconto
Vol. 16, Narrativa, $10.00

LEWIS TURCO
Shaking the Family Tree
Vol. 15, Poetry, $9.00

LUIGI RUSTICHELLI, ED.
Seminario sulla drammaturgia
Vol. 14, Theater/Essays, $10.00

FRED L. GARDAPHÈ
Moustache Pete is Dead!
Vol. 13, Oral literature, $10.00

JONE GAILLARD CORSI
Il libretto d'autore, 1860–1930
Vol. 12, Criticism, $17.00

HELEN BAROLINI
Chiaroscuro: Essays of Identity
Vol. 11, Essays, $15.00

T. PICARAZZI & W. FEINSTEIN, EDS.
An African Harlequin in Milan
Vol. 10, Theater/Essays, $15.00

JOSEPH RICAPITO
Florentine Streets and Other Poems
Vol. 9, Poetry, $9.00

FRED MISURELLA
Short Time
Vol. 8, Novella, $7.00

NED CONDINI
Quartettsatz
Vol. 7, Poetry, $7.00

A. J. TAMBURRI, ED. & M. J. BONA, INTROD.
Fuori: Essays by Italian/American
Lesbians and Gays
Vol. 6, Essays, $10.00

ANTONIO GRAMSCI
P. VERDICCHIO, TRANS. & INTROD.
The Southern Question
Vol. 5, Social Criticism, $5.00

DANIELA GIOSEFFI
Word Wounds and Water Flowers
Vol. 4, Poetry, $8.00

WILEY FEINSTEIN
Humility's Deceit: Calvino Reading
Ariosto Reading Calvino
Vol. 3, Criticism, $10.00

PAOLO A. GIORDANO, ED.
Joseph Tusiani:
Poet, Translator, Humanist
Vol. 2, Criticism, $25.00

ROBERT VISCUSI
Oration Upon the Most Recent Death
of Christopher Columbus
Vol. 1, Poetry, $3.00

www.ingramcontent.com/pod-product-compliance
Lightning Source LLC
Chambersburg PA
CBHW022341040426

42449CB00006B/668